Space Explorer

THE EARTH

Patricia Whitehouse

Heinemann Library
Chicago, Illinois

© 2004 Heinemann Library
a division of Reed Elsevier Inc.
Chicago, Illinois

Customer Service 888-454-2279

Visit our website at www.heinemannlibrary.com

Designed by Heinemann Library
Printed in China by South China Printing.

08 07 06 05 04
10 9 8 7 6 5 4 3 2 1

Library of Congress Cataloging-in-Publication Data
Whitehouse, Patricia, 1958-
  Earth / Patricia Whitehouse.
      v. cm. -- (Space explorer)
  Includes bibliographical references and index.
  Contents: Looking at Earth -- A big blue marble -- Earth's axis or the moving Earth -- Day and night -- Useful photographs -- Clouds and atmosphere -- Hurricanes -- Oceans and ice -- Continents -- Deserts and mountains -- Volcanoes erupting -- City lights -- As seen from space -- Amazing Earth facts.
    ISBN 1-4034-5150-8 (lib. bdg.) -- ISBN 1-4034-5654-2 (pbk.)
  1. Earth--Juvenile literature. [1. Earth.] I. Title. II. Series.
  QB631.4.W48 2004
  550--dc22

                                    2003026761

Acknowledgments
The author and publishers are grateful to the following for permission to reproduce copyright material:

Cover photograph: Geospace/Science Photo Library

p. 4 Russell Illiq/Getty Image/Photodisc; p. 5 NASA; p. 6 NASA; p. 7 NASA; p. 9 Robert Glusic/Getty Image/Photodisc; p. 10 Stock Trek; p. 11 Stock Trek; p. 12 Photolink/Getty Image/Photodisc; p. 13 Science Photo Library; p. 14 NASA; p. 15 Stock Trek; p. 16 C.Lee/Photolink; p. 17 NASA; p. 18 Corbis; p. 19 CNES; p. 20 Stock Trek; p. 21 Jacques Descloitres/NOAA; p. 22 NASA; p. 23 NASA; p. 24 Corbis; p. 25 NASA; p. 26 Photolink/Getty Image/Photodisc; p. 27 Corbis; p. 28 NASA

Every effort has been made to contact copyright holders of any material reproduced in this book. Any omissions will be rectified in subsequent printings if notice is given to the publisher.

Special thanks to Geza Gyuk of the Adler Planetarium for his comments in preparation of this book.

Some words are shown in bold, **like this.** You can find out what they mean by looking in the glossary.

Contents

Looking at Earth

We all live on planet Earth. Look around you, what can you see? You see only a tiny part of Earth because it is so large.

From Earth we can see only a small part of our planet.

This is a different view of Earth. It shows what it looks like from space.

A Big Blue Marble

Twelve **astronauts** have seen Earth from the surface of the Moon. One astronaut said that from space Earth looks like a big blue marble.

A view of Earth from the Moon.

Looking at Earth from the cargo
bay of a space shuttle.

Hundreds of astronauts have seen Earth
from spacecrafts and space stations.
Many people on Earth have seen
satellite images of Earth, too.

The Earth is always moving. We cannot feel it, though. It spins on its **axis.** It takes 24 hours for Earth to turn around once on its axis.

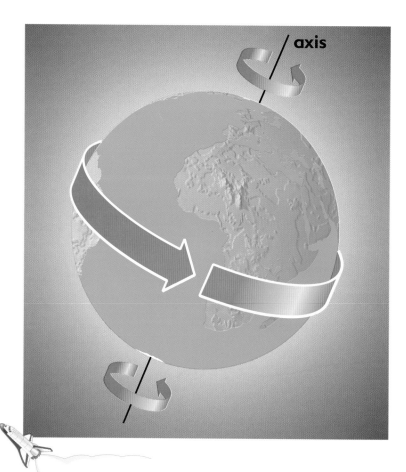

Earth's axis is an imaginary line that runs through the middle of Earth.

As Earth spins, people's view of the sky changes. This is because they are looking out at different parts of space.

As Earth spins, different parts move in and out of the Sun's light. This is how day and night happen.

Day and Night

From space, it is easy to see which part of Earth is in sunlight. The edge of sunlight is where day is beginning or ending.

It is daytime on the side of Earth facing the Sun.

As Earth spins, day changes to night and night to day in different places on Earth. While it is night on one side of Earth, it is day on the other.

As day begins in some places on Earth, night begins in others.

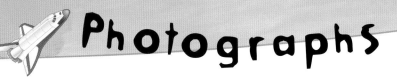

Photographs

Satellites take pictures of Earth from space. Scientists use these photographs to learn more about Earth.

Scientists look at satellite photos of Earth to see changes in its temperature and weather.

12

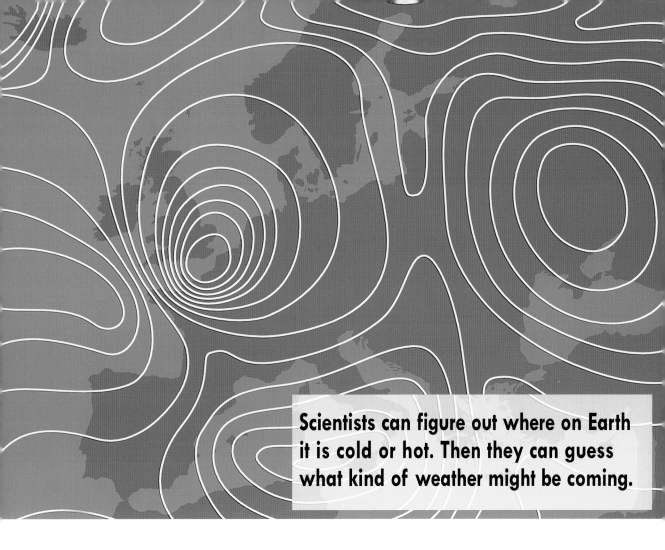

Scientists can figure out where on Earth it is cold or hot. Then they can guess what kind of weather might be coming.

Some satellite photographs show buildings and streets. These photos are used to make maps. Other satellite photographs show changes in the weather. They are used to help **forecast** the weather.

The Earth is covered with a layer of **gases** called the **atmosphere.** Almost all life on Earth needs these gases to live. From space, Earth's atmosphere looks thin and blue.

The shape and type of clouds can help show what kind of weather is coming.

The atmosphere is full of white clouds. The clouds change and sometimes disappear as they move across Earth. **Meteorologists** watch the changes to **forecast** the weather.

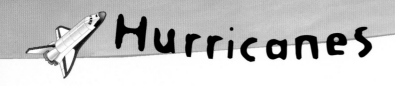 Hurricanes

A hurricane is a type of storm. The strong winds and heavy rains can damage buildings and trees. **Meteorologists** use pictures from space to **forecast** when a hurricane will happen.

eye of the hurricane

This photo shows a hurricane from space. The hurricane clouds spin around the eye of the hurricane. In the eye, the weather is calm.

Satellites take photographs of Earth's oceans to show their different **temperatures.** The temperature of water in the oceans affects weather patterns on Earth.

This satellite photograph shows temperatures as different colors. The red is hot, the purple is cool.

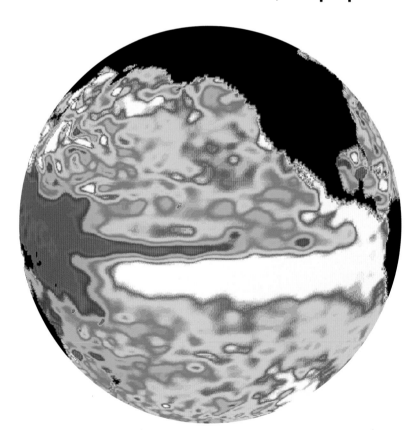

This is a satellite picture of an iceberg near Antarctica.

Some oceans are covered with ice.
The Arctic Ocean is covered with ice
all year. Photos of the Arctic Ocean
can show how the ice changes.

Continents

A continent is a very large area of land. Sometimes continents include many countries. The Earth has seven continents. From space, each continent is easy to see.

In this satellite photograph, North and South America can be seen.

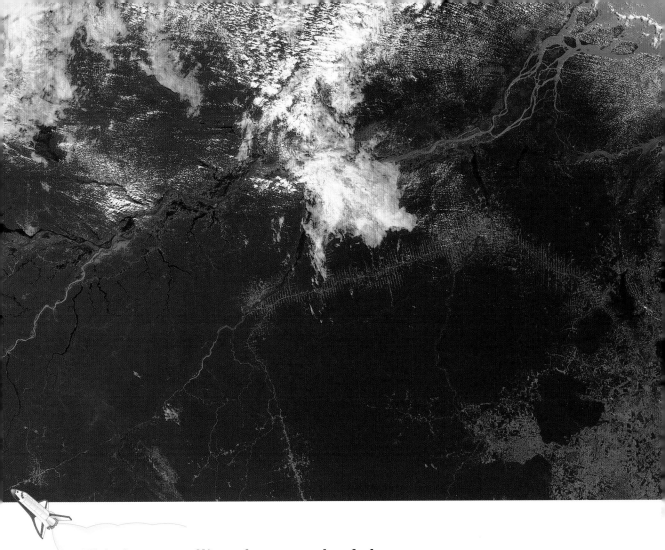

**This is a satellite photograph of the
Amazon rain forest, in South America.**

Satellites can take photographs of a
whole continent, or just a small part.
From space, a forest on a continent
looks like a green carpet.

21

Deserts and Mountains

Deserts are places on Earth that do not get much rain. Many deserts are sandy and have very few plants.

This is a satellite photograph of the Sahara Desert, in Africa. The ridges are sand dunes.

This is a satellite photograph of the mountains in Europe called the Alps. The white part of this photo is snow.

Mountains form the tallest parts of Earth. On Earth, mountains tower above us, but from space, they look like wrinkled paper.

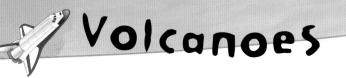 Volcanoes

A volcano looks like a mountain. But hot **gases,** lava, and ash flow out of volcanoes when they **erupt.** Some volcano eruptions can be seen from space.

Lava is liquid rock that is pushed to Earth's surface when a volcano erupts.

Satellites in space take photographs of the clouds of ash that come out of volcanoes. These clouds of smoke are carried in the wind and may be seen for days.

A cloud of smoke erupts from Kliuchevskoi, a volcano in Russia.

City Lights

At night, cities make a lot of light because of buildings and street lights. People in cities can see few stars in the night sky because of this **light pollution.**

City lights can be seen from space. Light areas show where cities are across Earth. Dark places are areas that have no large cities.

A **space probe** traveled to Mars to take pictures on the planet. It also took a photograph of Earth on the way.

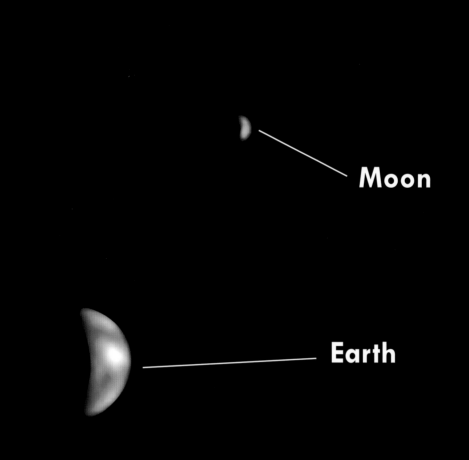

Moon

Earth

If a **satellite** near the planet Jupiter could take a photograph of Earth, it would look like only a tiny dot of light.

From Jupiter, Earth would look similar to the stars we can see at night.

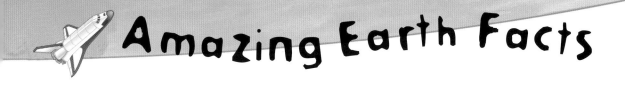

Amazing Earth Facts

The Earth is not perfectly round. It is flatter at the poles and wider in the middle.

The first **satellite** image of Earth used for **forecasting** weather was sent from space on April 1, 1960.

You can see satellites that take photographs of Earth moving across the night sky. They look like tiny points of light.

Glossary

astronaut person who goes into space

atmosphere layer of gases around a planet

axis imaginary line that runs through Earth from the North Pole to the South Pole

erupt burst out of

forecast guess what is going to happen in the future

gas airlike material that is not solid or liquid

light pollution light that does not allow the night sky to be clearly seen

meteorologist scientist who studies the weather

satellite object that moves around a planet or a moon

space probe spacecraft used to explore space

temperature how hot or cold something is

More Books to Read

Ganeri, Anita, *Day and Night (Nature's Patterns)*. Chicago: Heinemann Library, 2004.

Hughes, Monica. *Weather Patterns (Nature's Patterns)*. Chicago: Heinemann Library, 2004.

Whitehouse, Patricia. *Space Equipment (Space Explorer)*, Chicago: Heinemann Library, 2004.

Index